First published in Great Britain in 2016 by Wayland

Copyright © Wayland, 2016

Editor: Nicola Edwards
Design: Kevin Knight

Artwork by Tim Hutchinson

ISBN: 978 0 7502 9998 5
10 9 8 7 6 5 4 3 2 1

Wayland, an imprint of
Hachette Children's Group
Part of Hodder and Stoughton
Carmelite House
50 Victoria Embankment
London EC4Y 0DZ

An Hachette UK Company
www.hachette.co.uk
www.hachettechildrens.co.uk

Printed and bound in China

Picture acknowledgements:
All photographic images courtesy of Shutterstock except
for p14b Getty Images (Myung J. Chan/Los Angeles Times);
p20t Alamy (© Hugh Peterswald/Pacific Press/Alamy Live News);
p23t Alamy (© Martin Berry/Alamy Stock Photo); p25t Alamy
(© Lenscap/Alamy Stock Photo); p30 Floriana/Flickr

Every attempt has been made to clear copyright.
Should there be any inadvertent omission,
please apply to the publisher for rectification.

HOW TO DESIGN THE WORLD'S BEST
SKATEPARK
IN 10 SIMPLE STEPS

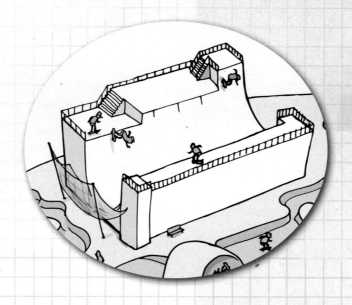

PAUL MASON

WAYLAND
www.waylandbooks.co.uk

CONTENTS

DESIGNING THE WORLD'S BEST SKATEPARK

Imagine your school's headteacher, or your local council, or even an eccentric millionaire giving you some land and a sackful of money, and telling you to build a skatepark. You'd definitely want it to be the best skatepark in the world – but how do you go about designing THAT?

You start by collecting together three basic design tools:
1) Your imagination
2) A pencil
3) A piece of paper
You will also need an eraser... no design is ever perfect first go! In fact, one of the most important skills when designing something is making changes and improvements.

RESEARCH

The next step is to gather information about what makes a great skatepark. Try to get information from all types of skateboarder and BMXer. This will help you design a skatepark that is popular with everyone.

There are lots of places you could find information about top skateparks:

1) Yourself
If have ever been to a skatepark, you probably already have some ideas about the features you and your friends most enjoy.

2) The Internet
Researching on the Internet means you can find out about skateparks all around the world. Remember, though: not all information on the Internet is reliable. Look for information from experts, such as magazines or famous riders. You could try search terms such as:
world + best + skatepark
top ten skateparks
best skatepark in [Europe] [then any other regions or countries you are interested in]
   Do not use only the usual search engines, such as Google. Look for specialist skateboard engines, such as skateboarddirectory.com. In fact, one of your first searches could be for 'skateboard search engine'. Specialist search engines usually produce very different results from non-specialist ones.

Skateparks are expensive to build, so yours will need to attract plenty of skateboarders and BMXers to justify the cost. Making it the best skatepark around will help!

Skateparks are not only for skateboarders: BMXers, rollerbladers and others use them too. Yours will need to be popular with everyone.

Open-air concrete parks like this one have been popular since the 1970s.

3) Books and magazines

Skateboarding and BMX publications often have articles about top parks around the world. A visit to your local library would be a good place to start.

4) Ask around!

Do any of your classmates, friends on social media or family go to skateparks? Ask them what they think makes a great one. If you make a list of questions to ask everyone, you will be able to compare people's views about the same things.

WORK IT OUT!

Plan a skater/BMXer survey to discover which skatepark features people think are most fun.

Your research will have revealed some features from top-ranked skateparks. Ask the people doing your survey what they think of these.

Pages 6 and 7 might give you a few more ideas.

WHAT MAKES THE IDEAL SKATEPARK?

A survey of skateboarders and BMXers is a great way to find out what people think makes a top skatepark. The questions and answers on this page and the next are an example of the kind of questions you could ask. They might also give you some ideas for things to put into a dream skatepark.

Skating the lip of a bowl is always popular with good skaters.

SURVEY FACTS

SURVEY NUMBER: 210
SOURCE: Internet skatepark fan sites
LOCATIONS: Worldwide
AGES: All

1 *How old are you?*
a) 0-9 years — 17
b) 10-13 years — 61
c) 14-17 years — 78
d) 18 and over — 54

2 *Are you a skateboarder or a BMXer?*
Skateboarder — 157
BMXer — 53

3 *What level of ability are you?*
a) Beginner — 36
b) Lower intermediate — 70
c) Higher intermediate — 63
d) Expert — 41

4 *Would you ever take part in, or watch, a skateboard or BMX competition?*
a) Compete and watch — 22
b) Watch, not compete — 59
c) Neither — 109
d) Not sure — 20

5 *When at a skatepark, which area do you use most often?*
a) Street — 71
b) Vert/ramp — 73
c) Flatland/slalom — 21
d) Longboard — 44

6 *Do you normally visit more than one area of the skatepark?*
Yes — 203
No — 7

WORK IT OUT!

When designing the skatepark, remember the skill level of the people who will be using it. For example, if you design a skatepark with 80% advanced-level features, but 75% of the users are beginners, the skatepark will not be a success.

Use the survey results for question 2 to work out what percentage of beginner, intermediate and advanced users there will be. For example:

36 of the 210 skaters are beginners. To make this into a percentage, calculate:

$36 \div 210 \times 100 = 17.14$

To the nearest whole number, 17% of the skaters will be beginners. You can check the other answers on page 31.

7 If so, which is your usual second area?
a) Street
b) Vert/ramp   61
c) Flatland/slalom   72
d) Longboard   51
                                19

8 Which skatepark features do you like most? (You can pick up to three.)
a) Bowl
b) Half pipe   73
c) Quarter pipe   62
d) Mini ramp   44
e) Hubbas   69
f) Funbox   58
g) Grinds, kerbs, ledges   63
h) Snake run   66
h) Flatland   48
                                33

WORK IT OUT!

How many skaters live near your own skatepark site?

Researchers have found that 4.6 in 100 people will go skateboarding some time in the next year.

4.6 in 100 is the same as:

0.46 in 10, which is the same as:

0.046 in 1

So if you multiply the population of your local area* by 0.046, you will have a rough idea of how many skateboarders there are.

Possible reasons to adjust your figure:

Warm, sunny climate add 20%

Cold, wet climate subtract 20%

Large number of young people add 15%

Large number of older people subtract 25%

There is a working-out example on page 31.

*For example your city, or every settlement within 20 minutes' journey. Your local government office or town council will know how many people live in specific areas.

DREAM DESIGN

After your research into the world's top skateparks, plus the user survey on pages 6 and 7, you are probably bursting with skatepark-design ideas! It's time to start sketching out your dream design.

Remember: the park has to be fun for ALL kinds of skaters. Beginners, experts and everyone in between should be welcome. You need space for street skaters, vert skaters, freestyle experts and longboard riders.

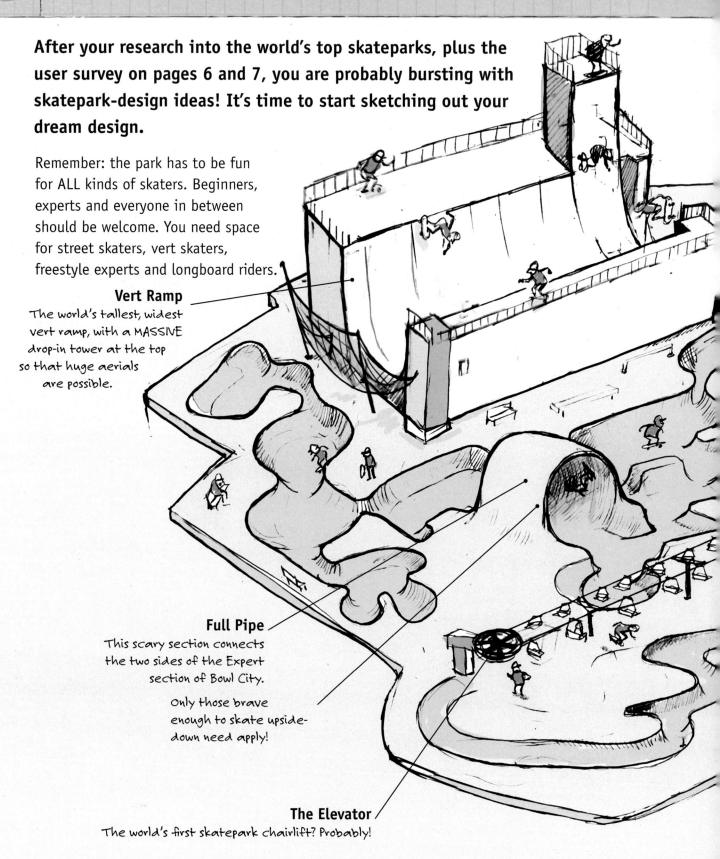

Vert Ramp
The world's tallest, widest vert ramp, with a MASSIVE drop-in tower at the top so that huge aerials are possible.

Full Pipe
This scary section connects the two sides of the Expert section of Bowl City.

Only those brave enough to skate upside-down need apply!

The Elevator
The world's first skatepark chairlift? Probably!

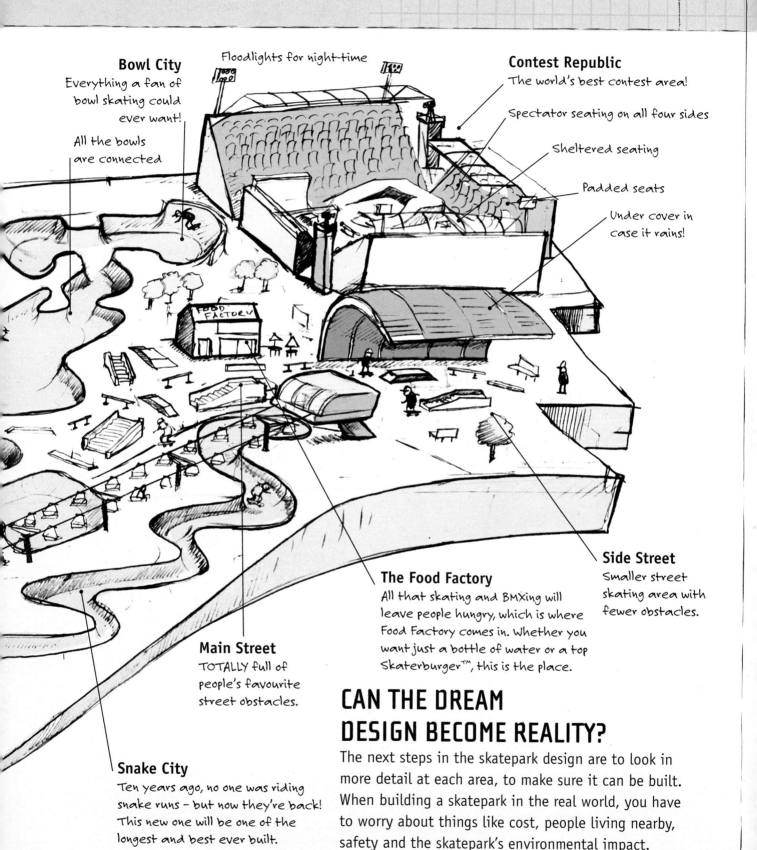

Bowl City
Everything a fan of bowl skating could ever want!

All the bowls are connected

Floodlights for night-time

Contest Republic
The world's best contest area!

Spectator seating on all four sides

Sheltered seating

Padded seats

Under cover in case it rains!

Side Street
Smaller street skating area with fewer obstacles.

The Food Factory
All that skating and BMXing will leave people hungry, which is where Food Factory comes in. Whether you want just a bottle of water or a top Skaterburger™, this is the place.

Main Street
TOTALLY full of people's favourite street obstacles.

Snake City
Ten years ago, no one was riding snake runs – but now they're back! This new one will be one of the longest and best ever built.

CAN THE DREAM DESIGN BECOME REALITY?
The next steps in the skatepark design are to look in more detail at each area, to make sure it can be built. When building a skatepark in the real world, you have to worry about things like cost, people living nearby, safety and the skatepark's environmental impact.

BOWL CITY

Bowl City is going to be one of the biggest and best bowl-skating areas ever. The original plan shows one huge group of interlinked bowls. Within this, there are separate areas for beginners, intermediate and advanced users. But will the dream design work in real life?

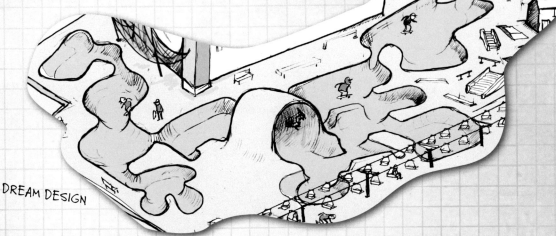

DREAM DESIGN

Research Note

Anyone designing a big building project has to do something called a 'risk assessment'. Experts look at the design and decide whether anything is too dangerous, and risks people being hurt.

Depending on what is being built, some risk is OK. Skateboarding and BMX are dangerous activities – it would be impossible to make them risk-free. But even a skatepark design has to be checked for dangers that could be avoided.

Bowl areas need plenty of run-off space – people sometimes leave the bowl at high speed!

THE RISK ASSESSMENT

The risk assessment says that adaptations are needed to the Dream Design:
1) The way the bowls are linked means there is a risk of skaters colliding at high speed
2) Safety zones at least 2m wide are needed at the edges of all the bowls.

Research Note

Skateboarders have developed a set of rules for vert skating:

Everyone is equal

Everyone is allowed, whatever they ride, and everyone has to follow the rules.

One at a time

Only one rider at a time on any ramp.

Wait your turn

No pushing in: do not drop in before someone who has been waiting longer.

No stopping in red zones

Never stand anywhere that's in the way of someone using the bowl or ramp.

Don't be a hog

Even if you're able to do a 5-minute bowl ride, don't! Give everyone else a chance to have a turn.

WORK IT OUT!

Design an eye-catching poster to go at every drop-in in Bowl City.

The poster should be based on the skaters' vert-skating rules (see the research notes panel).

If you use a combination of words and images, people who cannot read English will find it easier to get the message.

THE FINAL DESIGN

The best way to make the design safe is to separate the bowls into three areas. One area will be for beginners, the second for lower intermediates and the third for upper intermediate and advanced skaters.

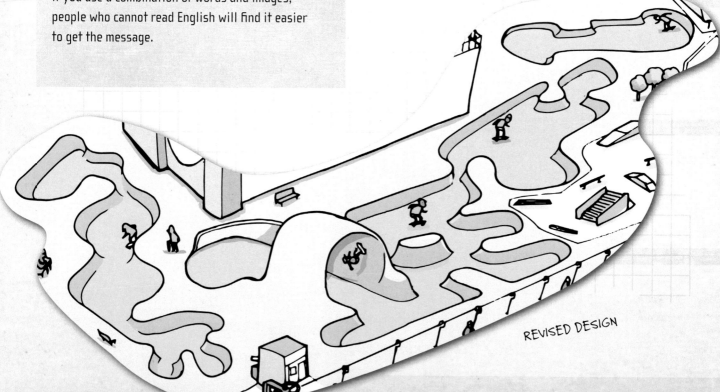

REVISED DESIGN

FULL PIPE

The Dream Design shows an open-ended full pipe right in the heart of the Expert zone. The great thing about this is that skaters and BMXers can get into it from either end of the pipe. They can do a full loop, then skate out on the other side.

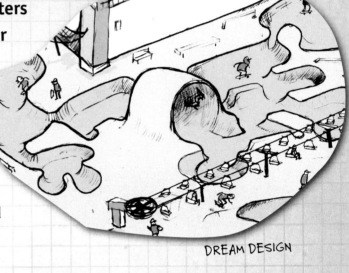

DREAM DESIGN

A LOOPY DESIGN?

Unfortunately, the risk assessment (see page 10) has said that changes will be needed to the design. There is a big problem. Two people could enter the pipe from each end at the exact-same moment, without seeing each other. What would happen if they met halfway, at the top of the loop?

KER-RUNCH

TRAFFIC LIGHTS AND RUN-OFF ZONES

There are two ways the problem with the Full Pipe design could be solved:

1) A traffic-light system

Red and green lights could be placed above the entrances. If one side was green, the other would automatically be red. A red light would mean you cannot enter. Green would mean go!

2) A run-off zone

The design could be changed so that you can only get into the Full Pipe from one end. The other end would be a run-off zone, where skaters could stop before dropping into one of the other bowls.

WORK IT OUT!

Make a decision about the best way to make the Full Pipe as safe as possible.

It might help to make a table showing the plus and minus points of each option. The table could start like this:

	Plus points	Minus points
Traffic light	Skaters can enter from either side	
Run-off		Only one entrance

Which option has the most pluses and the fewest minuses? Can you find a plus point for one of the options that the alternative cannot match? Or a minus point that means one option cannot be used?

Once you have thought about it yourself, you can find out more on page 31.

This full pipe has a closed end, making it unlikely that two people could hit each other while using it.

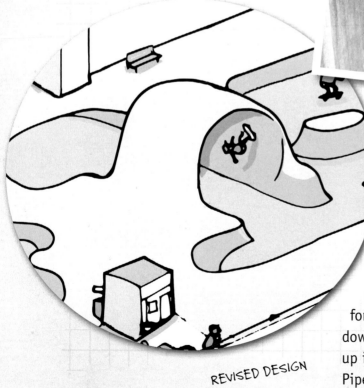

REVISED DESIGN

THE FINAL DESIGN

The final design is for a run-off system. This option has one massive advantage: it is impossible for two people to enter from opposite sides without seeing each other.

For a bit of added fun, the only way to get into Full Pipe will be through a short tunnel leading from the main area for advanced users. The tunnel will slope downhill slightly, to stop people coming back up it. Whizzing through it and into the Full Pipe is going to be a good challenge.

VERT RAMP

The original design shows an enormous vert ramp with a massive drop-in at the top. The drop-in was planned to be even bigger than Bob Burnquist's 20m-high megaramp. (Burnquist is a professional skateboarder who built the world's biggest megaramp in his back garden!).

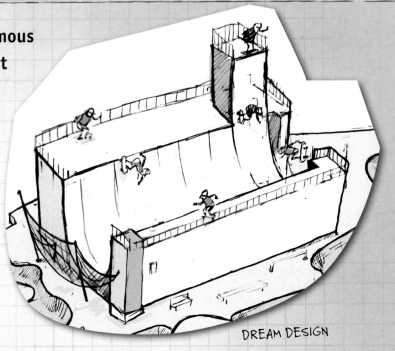

DREAM DESIGN

HOW MUCH SPEED IS TOO MUCH?

On Burnquist's megaramp, skaters regularly reach speeds of 90kph. On a taller ramp, they would go even faster. Some might even get close to the world-record for skateboard speed: 129.94kph!

Crashing at such high speeds could cause terrible injuries, or even kill you. It is too risky for a skatepark where beginners are welcome.

HOW BIG IS TOO BIG?

The huge vert ramp in the original design had high, steep sides. These are great for total experts – but only one in five people in the survey were experts. Lots of the others would probably watch them using the ramp, but be scared off actually using it.

Bob Burnquist built his megaramp after riding one at the X-Games. Burnquist thought the X-Games ramp was not quite big enough – so he went home and built a bigger one in his back garden.

A wide, low vert ramp is ideal for beginners who want to build their confidence – and for experts who want to practise new tricks.

THE FINAL DESIGN

The final design will still have a drop-in, but it will not be as high. The experts will now drop in from a platform that is 3m above the edge of the ramp. This part of the ramp will still have steep, tall sides.

Further down, the ramp will have lower sides and be wider, to make it easier for intermediate and beginner skaters.

WORK IT OUT!

The redesigned Vert Ramp is going to be a big feature of the skatepark. An advert is needed to let people know about it – and the advert needs a cartoon of the ramp in action.

Base your cartoon on a model of the Vert Ramp. To make this, start with a sheet of paper and the bottom part of an old shoe box, with one end cut out. Lay the paper across the shoe box, then use the ends to push it down into the box. Take care not to make a fold in the paper.

Keep pushing down until the paper's shape looks like the shape of a vert ramp. The sides should be vertical and the bottom will be flat, with a curved slope between them.

When it looks right, stick the paper in place with some tape and start drawing!

Beginner zone
Sides lower, but still vertical

Expert zone
Steep, high sides

Intermediate zone
Sides are lower

REVISED DESIGN

MAIN STREET

The original design shows every concrete street feature a skater or BMXer could dream of. There are rails, walls, funboxes, three different-sized hubbas, kerbs and ledges for grinds, and a flatland area to one side.

The risk assessment (see the research note panel on page 10) says that the design could be built exactly as planned. However, people designing big building projects also have to have an 'environmental assessment' done. This is a report on the effect the building will have on the environment. The report says that building all the street features from concrete would have a big impact on the environment. It suggests that wood might be a better building material.

Will building from wood, like in the photo above right, do less damage to the environment than using concrete, as in the photo above? Some research and some sums will help you work out the answer.

Research Note

All building materials have an 'energy cost'. This is the amount of energy it usually takes to produce, transport and build with them. This process also produces a gas called carbon dioxide (CO_2), which is bad for the environment.

Typical skatepark building materials are concrete and wood. Experts have calculated these energy costs and CO_2 figures for each:

	Concrete	Wood
Energy cost per square metre:	290kJ	80kJ
CO_2 produced per square metre:	27kg	4kg

WORK IT OUT!

From an environmental viewpoint, is wood a better building material than concrete?

Make a decision based on three things:

1) The amount of energy that will be used to construct the street-skating areas

2) The amount of carbon dioxide (CO_2) that will be released

3) How long each building material will last

The street features in Main Street and Side Street will have a surface area of 1,200m² in total. The facts in the research note panel will help you work out what your decision should be.

For example:

1) Energy used

If building with concrete uses 290kJ of energy per square metre, and the street area is going to be 1,200m², the amount of energy used is:

290 x 1,200 = 348,000kJ

Once you have worked out the figures for each material, there is one more calculation to do. Concrete lasts longer than wood. If the wood park will last 15 years before being replaced and the concrete will last 45 years, which has the lowest environmental impact per year?

You can check the answers on page 31.

THE FINAL DESIGN

As many features as possible in the street area will be made of wood. This is not only is it better for the environment – when the wood has to be replaced, it will be a chance to update the whole area.

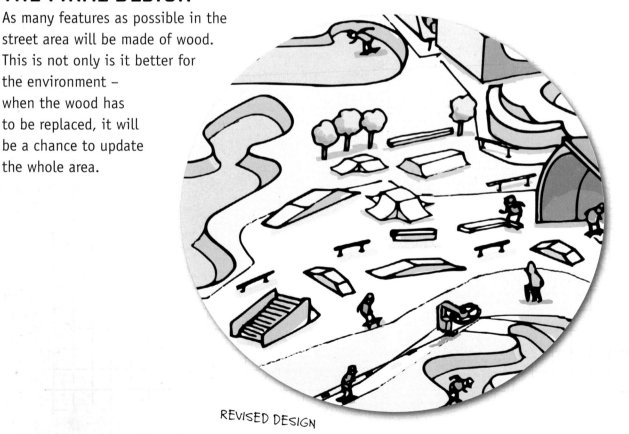

REVISED DESIGN

SIDE STREET

Even in a dream skatepark, it will sometimes rain!
Water can make outdoor skatepark areas
slippery and dangerous. It also
damages a skateboard's bearings.
The under-cover Side Street
area will give everyone
somewhere to go when
it is raining or damp.

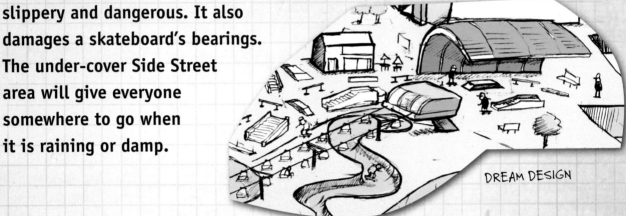

DREAM DESIGN

POSSIBLE ALTERATIONS

Side Street's features will now be built mainly
from wood, instead of concrete (see page 17 to
remind yourself about this decision). Apart from
that, are any other changes needed?

Cost savings

One of a designer's jobs is to create the best
possible design at the lowest possible cost.
At the moment, the Dream Design has two
roofed areas in the street zone: the roof over
Side Street, and the one over Food Factory.
Building one large roof would be less expensive
than building two separate ones.

Environmental impact

The skatepark will use water for flushing toilets,
cleaning, drinking, etc. The original plan was
for this water to come from pipes, like the
water in people's homes. But the environmental
impact report (see page 16) suggests collecting
rainwater from the skatepark's roofs, then
storing it for use later.

Research Note

These are average amounts of water
used for:

1) Flushing a toilet 6l
2) Having a shower 65.1l
3) Running a tap 1.9l per minute

Skating in the wet is dangerous
and can wreck your equipment.
An undercover area is especially
useful if you live somewhere rainy.

WORK IT OUT!

The skatepark is going to collect rainwater from its roofs. You need to work out how much water it will collect and what the water could be used for:

• There are two roof areas in the final design. One is over Side Street: it is 297m². The other is a smaller roof over part of the competition area: this is 118m².

• Throughout the year, the average rainfall is 783.2 l of water per sq m.

To work out how much rain will fall on each roof, multiply the size of the roof by the average rainfall figure.

Read the research note and use the information to work out what the water could be used for. For example, if the average toilet flush uses 6l of water, how many toilet flushes will the skatepark's roofs provide?

You can check your answers on page 31.

THE FINAL DESIGN

In the final design, Food Factory will be moved to a place next to Side Street. Both will be covered by the same roof. There are two design benefits to this change:

1) The cost of the street-skating area will be lower than before, because the builders will build one roof, instead of two.

2) It will be easier to collect rainwater from a single roof. Fewer pipes will be needed leading from the roof to the water storage.

REVISED DESIGN

CONTEST REPUBLIC

The Dream Design includes the world's best contest area. It has seating on four sides, with a roof over one of the spectator areas. There are floodlights, a warm-up area for the competitors to practise, camera platforms and every other facility you can imagine.

DREAM DESIGN

Contest Republic is going to cost a lot of money to build. All the seating, camera platforms and other facilities are more expensive than in the rest of the park. Before making a final decision, the designer needs to ask: is it worth it?

ADAPTING TO PEOPLE'S NEEDS

Designs only work well if they are what people want. It is clear from the user survey that not many of the skatepark's users are interested in contests. So spending a lot of money on the contest area is a bad idea. It would be better to spend the money on things people will actually use.

WORK IT OUT!

Look at the user survey from pages 6 and 7 to see what percentage of people are interested in taking part in and/or watching competitions:

You can remind yourself how to turn these numbers into percentages on page 7. Check your answers on page 31.

4) Would you ever take part in, or watch, a skateboard or BMX competition?
a) Compete and watch   22
b) Watch, not compete   59
c) Neither   109
d) Not sure   20

Live coverage of competitions can be streamed all over the world via the Internet.

Research Note

Skatepark contests can show off the park to millions of people. This is because hundreds of thousands of people watch skate and BMX contests online, either live streamed or on video sites.

The biggest-ever audiences for skateboard events include:

• A 2014 live broadcast of a street contest on TV, which had 1.7 million viewers.

• A 2015 contest that was watched on the Internet by 750,000 skate fans.

This means designing a contest area with camera platforms is a really good idea.

Pool-skating contests usually draw a crowd – especially if the sun is out.

THE FINAL DESIGN

The skatepark will still have a contest area. Over one-third of the people in the user survey enjoy watching contests, even if they do not want to take part in them. But in the final design, Contest Republic will lose all but one of its most expensive features:

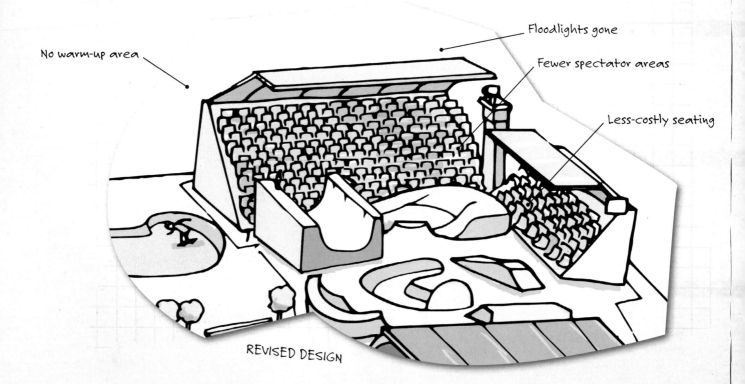

No warm-up area

Floodlights gone

Fewer spectator areas

Less-costly seating

REVISED DESIGN

THE ELEVATOR

The Dream Design has a ski-style chairlift taking skaters from the bottom of the park back to the higher level. Having this would mean they can ride down through the different zones, or do the Snake Run, then whizz back up on the chairlift instead of having to trudge up a path.

DREAM DESIGN

CHAIRLIFT TROUBLE

There are two problems with the Dream Design:
1) Chairlifts are normally used for skiing and snowboarding. In these, the skis and snowboards are safely strapped to the riders' feet. They cannot fall off. Skateboards are NOT strapped to the riders' feet. The risk of them being dropped from the chairlift is too great.
2) Chairlifts have turned out to be really expensive! Even with the savings that have been made to Contest Republic, it would be better to find a cheaper way of getting people back to the top.

Research Note

These three systems are all used in ski resorts to move skiers and snowboarders back to the top of a slope:

1) Button lifts, where a little disc on the end of a pole is fitted between your legs to drag you uphill.

Estimated cost: £750.00 per metre

2) Rope drags, where you hold on to a moving rope to be pulled along.

Estimated cost: £172.00 per metre

3) Moving walkways like the ones in some shopping centres and airports (in ski resorts these are called 'magic carpets').

Estimated cost: £595.00 per metre

A chairlift in a ski resort whisks people up the mountain.

WORK IT OUT!

Use the research note to work out the best way of getting people back to the higher area of the skatepark.

The method you decide on will need to move people 53m uphill. Make the decision based on these questions:

• Is it good for skaters and BMXers?

• Is there any danger to other users?

• How much does it cost?

You could draw up a table like this to work out your results:

Method	Good for skaters and BMXers?	Dangerous to other users?	Cost (price per metre x 53)
Button lift	No		
Rope drag	Not ideal for BMXers		
Conveyor belt			

You can check your working-out on page 31.

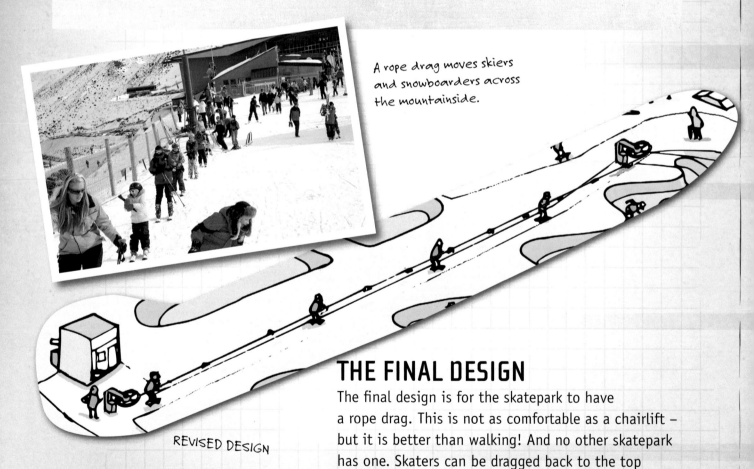

A rope drag moves skiers and snowboarders across the mountainside.

REVISED DESIGN

THE FINAL DESIGN

The final design is for the skatepark to have a rope drag. This is not as comfortable as a chairlift – but it is better than walking! And no other skatepark has one. Skaters can be dragged back to the top standing on their boards. Confident BMXers will tuck the rope under their arm, then press it down on the handlebars for extra grip. The rest will have to pedal!

SNAKE CITY

The snake run is one of the most unusual features of the Dream Design. It goes downhill from a built-up start hill. There are high banks and wider sections where the skaters can do tricks. Runs like this were last popular in the 1970s, but are becoming fashionable again. Longboard skaters particularly like them.

DREAM DESIGN

Research Note

Two of the world's most famous snake runs are:

• Kona Skatepark, Florida

An original snake run at possibly the world's oldest skatepark. The Kona run ends in a massive bowl claimed to be the biggest in any skatepark, anywhere.

• Camp Woodward, Pennsylvania.

At 350m, Camp Woodward's run is one of the longest anywhere. A complete contrast to Kona, it has all sorts of modern skate obstacles built in.

ADAPTATIONS NEEDED?

Things are looking good for the original design!
1) The safety report does not suggest any changes. The run is suitable for everyone. Beginners can go slowly down the middle of the run. Experts can swoop up and down the sides to pick up speed.
2) The environmental assessment does ask whether the run could be made of wood instead of concrete (see pages 16 and 17). This is not possible, though. The smooth, continuous curves of a snake run can only be built of concrete.

There is just one problem: the start hill is a bit too high! People living nearby have complained that the skaters and BMXers will be able to see into their homes. The hill will have to be 1m lower than planned.

WORK IT OUT!

The snake run was going to be 209m long, with a vertical drop of 9m. This means the run would have dropped 4.3cm per metre. You work out the drop per metre like this:

9 ÷ 209 = 0.043

0.043m = 4.3cm

Now that the start hill is going to be lower, the vertical drop will be 8m instead of 9m. Can you work out how long the run would need to be to have the same drop per metre?

Check the answer on page 31.

The snake run at Rom skatepark in Essex, England – which claims to be the oldest skatepark in the country.

THE FINAL DESIGN

In the final design, the snake run is a little shorter. About 10% has been cut from the middle part, and the start hill is 1m lower. Apart from that, the run is just as planned.

REVISED DESIGN

FOOD FACTORY

The original design for the skatepark shows a snack bar called Food Factory alongside Main Street. It will serve drinks, snacks and fresh-cooked food to hungry skaters. Round the back are some toilets. The location has already moved to Side Street – apart from that, should any other changes be made?

DREAM DESIGN

RAINWATER SHOWERS?

Food Factory's roof will collect rainwater for use in the skatepark. This could be used to provide showers for hot, sweaty skaters. But the MOST important use of the water is for flushing the skatepark's toilets. Will there be enough water left over for showers?

WORK IT OUT!

The park is expected to have an average of 200 visitors a day on weekdays, and 750 on weekends. Experts calculate that each visitor will go to the toilet twice per visit. How many times will the toilet be flushed in a year?

Compare this number with what you worked out about water collection from the roofs (see page 19) to see if there is enough.

You can check your answers on p.31.

WHAT'S ON THE MENU?

Food Factory will have to provide the skatepark's users with tasty food to be a success. But the food will also have to provide them with the right kinds of nutrition. Otherwise they will not digest their food properly, have enough energy, or recover quickly from the demands of skating and BMX.

Skating and BMXing are high-energy activities – no one can do them all day without taking some food on board.

Research Note

Food can be divided into groups.
The main ones are:

• Carbohydrates
These provide energy. They can be found in potatoes, rice, pasta and bread.

• Proteins
These help the body grow and repair itself. Sources include meat, fish, beans and eggs.

• Fats
These provide energy and help growth. The most common sources of fat are dairy products and deep-fried foods.

• Fibre
This helps the body to digest food. It is found in cereals, some bread, fruit and vegetables.

• Vitamins and minerals
These keep your body working properly, and help build teeth, bones, nerves and brain. Fruit and vegetables are a good source.

WORK IT OUT!

Design a menu for hungry skaters/BMXers.

The menu needs to have:

• Four snacks, such as a fruit selection or yoghurt and muesli
• Four bigger meals, such as a sandwich, burger or pot of salad
• Three drinks

Fizzy drinks are not allowed, and the menu should contain a mixture of ALL the food groups in the research note panel.

All that skating and BMXing will leave people hungry, which is where Food Factory comes in. Whether you want just a bottle of water or a top Skaterburger™, this is the place.

REVISED DESIGN

Every section of the skatepark's design has been examined, from Bowl City to how many times the toilets will be flushed every year. Changes have been made after reports from safety and environmental experts, local residents, engineers, and skateboarders and BMXers. Finally, the design is complete.

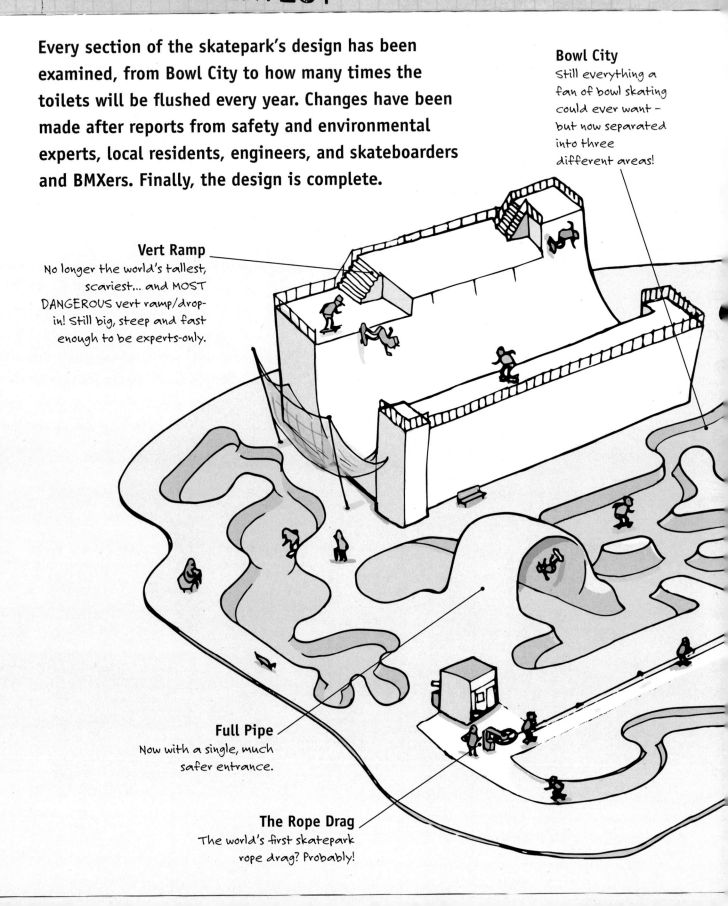

Bowl City
Still everything a fan of bowl skating could ever want – but now separated into three different areas!

Vert Ramp
No longer the world's tallest, scariest... and MOST DANGEROUS vert ramp/drop-in! Still big, steep and fast enough to be experts-only.

Full Pipe
Now with a single, much safer entrance.

The Rope Drag
The world's first skatepark rope drag? Probably!

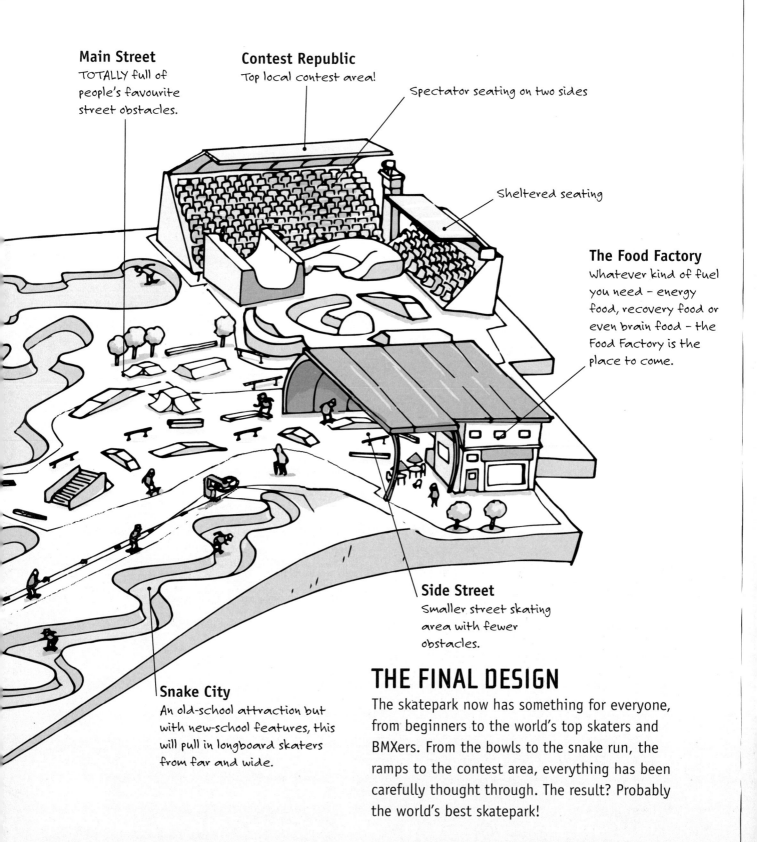

Main Street
TOTALLY full of people's favourite street obstacles.

Contest Republic
Top local contest area!

Spectator seating on two sides

Sheltered seating

The Food Factory
Whatever kind of fuel you need – energy food, recovery food or even brain food – the Food Factory is the place to come.

Snake City
An old-school attraction but with new-school features, this will pull in longboard skaters from far and wide.

Side Street
Smaller street skating area with fewer obstacles.

THE FINAL DESIGN
The skatepark now has something for everyone, from beginners to the world's top skaters and BMXers. From the bowls to the snake run, the ramps to the contest area, everything has been carefully thought through. The result? Probably the world's best skatepark!

THE WORLD'S TOP SKATEPARKS

The skatepark in this book is a great design – but it has not actually been built yet! If you want to visit one of the world's actual top skateparks, these are some that regularly feature in Top-Ten lists:

SMP

LOCATION: Shanghai, China
OPENED: 2005
If you look at the layout of SMP on www.smpskatepark.com, you will see that the basic layout inspired the skatepark in this book. It is one of the biggest and best skateparks in the world.

KONA SKATEPARK

LOCATION: Florida, USA
OPENED: 1977
Said to be the world's oldest outdoor skatepark, Kona's famous snake run was the inspiration for the same feature in this book.

CAMP WOODWARD

LOCATION: Pennsylvania, USA
OPENED: 1970
The original was in Pennsylvania, where it started as a gymnastics training camp before moving on to skateboarding, BMX and other sports. There are now Camp Woodwards in several locations around the USA. In 2010, Woodward Beijing, in China, opened its doors for the first time.

Built in an old train yard, Berlin's Skatehalle has one of the best street courses in Europe.

AMAZING SQUARE

LOCATION: Tokyo, Japan
OPENED: 2011
If Tokyo's skateboarders wake up at 3 a.m. desperate to go skating, this is where they go: Amazing Square is open 24 hours a day, every day. The brilliant skate facilities include a large vert ramp and street-skating area.

SKATEHALLE

LOCATION: Berlin, Germany
OPENED: mid-2000s
Despite the massive vert ramp and the 3-m wall ride, Skatehalle is a surprisingly good place for beginners to learn. Housed in an old train yard, it has one of the best street courses in Europe.

BLACK PEARL

LOCATION: Cayman Islands
OPENED: 2005
One of the biggest skateparks in the world, Black Pearl has facilities for just about every kind of skater. And if you get too hot in the Caribbean sunshine, the beach is a few minutes' walk away.

'WORK IT OUT' ANSWERS

for p.7 top

Results to the nearest whole number: 17% of users are beginner. 33% are lower intermediate. 30% are higher intermediate. 20% are expert.

for p.7 bottom

Working-out

Imagine you live in a town with 127,000 residents. Within 20 minutes' travel there are three smaller settlements, with 7,300, 7,100 and 2,100 residents.

So the total number of residents is 127,000 + 7,300 + 7,100 + 2,100 = 143,500.

143,500 x 0.046 = 6,601 skaters in the area

If you live somewhere warm and dry:

6,601 x 20% = 1,320 extra skaters

If there are lots of older people:

6,601 x 25% = 1,650 fewer skaters

for p.13

	Plus points:	Minus point:
Traffic light	• Skaters can enter from either side, adding variety • Skaters can use the pipe to go from one side of Bowl City to the other.	• Possible to enter from 'wrong' side by ignoring red light
Run-off	• Impossible for skaters to enter from different directions • Skaters have a safe slowing-down place • Skaters can use the pipe to go from one side of Bowl City to the other, with a resting place in between.	• Only one entrance, so less variety

With the traffic light, skaters and BMXers could still crash. The run-off zone makes crashes unlikely.

The run-off is the best option.

for p.17

	Energy used:	CO_2 released:	Per year of life:
Concrete:	348,000kJ	32,400kg	7,733kJ; 720 kg
Wood:	96,000kJ	4,800kg	6,400kJ; 320 kg

for p.19

The larger roof will collect

297 x 783.2 = 232,610.4l

The smaller roof will collect

118 x 783.2 = 92,417.6l

The total amount of water collected will be 325,028l

325,028l of water will provide 54,171 toilet flushes (the sum is 325,028 ÷ 6 = 54,171)

for p.20

10% would compete and watch a contest. 28% would watch but not compete. 52% would not compete or watch. 10% do not know.

This means that over half the people visiting the skatepark would not be interested in contests.

for p.23

Method	Good for skaters and BMXers?	Dangerous to other users?	Cost (price per metre x 53)
Button lift	No	No	750 x 53 = £39,750.00
Rope drag	Not ideal for BMXers	No	172 x 53 = £9,116.00
Moving walkway	Yes	No	595 x 53 = £31,535.00

The rope drag seems to be a good way to get people back to the top of the skatepark.

for p.25

You know the drop per metre you want (0.043m), and the total vertical drop (8m). To work out the length of the run:

8 ÷ 0.043 = 186m

To get the same drop (and speed!) the new design will have to be 186m long. That's 23m shorter than the original.

for p.26

The total visitors per week is 200 + 750 = 950.

There are 52 weeks in one year, so the total visitors in a year is 52 x 950 = 49,400.

If every visitor goes to the toilet twice, the total number of flushes per year will be 2 x 49,400 = 98,800.

Page 19 showed that the roof would collect enough water for 54,171 toilet flushes. The roofs will not collect enough water for toilet flushing – let alone for showers as well.

GLOSSARY

aerial jump or trick that involves leaving the ground

bearings tiny metal balls inside a wheel that allow it to turn smoothly

BMXer rider of a small, manoeuvrable bike with one gear

drop in start of a bowl or ramp ride

feature one part of a larger area or thing; for example, in a skatepark one of the features might be a mini-ramp

hubba section next to some stairs, with opportunities for grinds and other tricks

interlinked connected together

longboard skateboard with a longer deck and bigger, softer wheels than a normal board

loop curved path that goes from upright to vertical, then upside-down and back to upright

megaramp giant-sized skateboarding or BMX ramp

model a smaller version of an object or structure

new-school the newest and most fashionable way of doing something

nutrition food needed for growth and good health

old-school an old-style way of doing something

run-off space where it is safe and easy to slow down

snake run smooth, curving downhill run, made of concrete and usually ending in a bowl

™ sign that someone owns a word or name, and other people should not use it

transition link between parts of a ride

vertical drop difference in height between the start and the finish

vert skating skateboarding on bowls and ramps with vertical sections

warm-up get your body ready for exercise

INDEX